TIME
TOURS
SKY SMASH

Written by Steve Cole

Illustrated by Miriam Serafin

RISING ★ STARS

Hachette UK's policy is to use papers that are natural, renewable and recyclable products and made from wood grown in well-managed forests and other controlled sources. The logging and manufacturing processes are expected to conform to the environmental regulations of the country of origin.

ISBN: 9781398325609

Text © Steve Cole
Illustrations, design and layout © Hodder and Stoughton Ltd
First published in 2022 by Hodder & Stoughton Limited (for its Rising Stars imprint, part of the Hodder Education Group).
An Hachette UK Company
Carmelite House, 50 Victoria Embankment, London EC4Y 0DZ
www.risingstars-uk.com

Impression number 10 9 8 7 6 5 4 3 2 1
Year 2026 2025 2024 2023 2022

Author: Steve Cole
Series Editor: Tony Bradman
Commissioning Editor: Hamish Baxter
Illustrator: Miriam Serafin/Advocate Art
Educational Reviewer: Helen Marron
Design concept: Gary Kilpatrick
Page layouts: Rocket Design (East Anglia) Ltd
Editor: Amy Tyrer

With thanks to the schools that took part in the development of Reading Planet KS2, including: Ancaster CE Primary School, Ancaster; Downsway Primary School, Reading; Ferry Lane Primary School, London; Foxborough Primary School, Slough; Griffin Park Primary School, Blackburn; St Barnabas CE First & Middle School, Pershore; Tranmoor Primary School, Doncaster; and Wilton CE Primary School, Wilton.

A catalogue record for this title is available from the British Library.

Printed in the UK.

Orders: Please contact Hachette UK Distribution, Hely Hutchinson Centre, Milton Road, Didcot, Oxfordshire, OX11 7HH.

Telephone: (44) 01235 400555. Email: primary@hachette.co.uk.

MIX
Paper from responsible sources
FSC™ C104740
www.fsc.org

Contents

The story so far

By Ana Pirelli, aged 10

My brother, Rocco, and I were accidentally picked up by a time-travelling coach from the year 3000! The coach is owned by Time Tours.

With a boy from the future, called Ifan, and a robot tour guide, called Tori, we've travelled back in time to Victorian London ...

and Mayan Mexico.

But when we took our time pod to first-century Italy, we found trash-bots, owned by Time Tour's biggest competitors – Timely Trips, dumping rubbish there from the future!

We used a 'magna-drag' machine to make their coach super-magnetic! So as they left, they took the metal trash away with them – and our time pod, too!

Now, wherever the trash-bots go, we're going with them. Perhaps we will find out who's been telling them to dump rubbish in the past ... and we can do our best to stop them!

1 Prehistoric peril

"I think we're arriving!" cried Ana.

Rocco nodded. When the time pod travelled through time, flashes of light showed through the windows. Now, slowly, that view was changing. A leafy-green jungle was growing solid around them – along with tons of mangled metal, all of it stuck with magnetic power to the Timely Trips coach.

"Well, the trash-bots have brought us somewhere," said Rocco. "But where?"

"We are a long way back," said Tori in her squeaky robot voice. "The trash-bots have taken us 66 million years into the past – into what will one day be Mexico."

"Wow," said Ifan. "There were dinosaurs back then."

"I'd sooner meet a dinosaur than those trash-bots again," said Rocco. "I hope they don't realise we've hitched a ride with them."

"I think they will be more worried about how their time coach became super-magnetic," said Tori, "and took all that trash back through time."

"That would be thanks to our excellent work with their magna-drag machine," said Ana with a smile.

Even with the time pod's door closed, the sound of a loud clang and clatter carried from outside as all the scrap fell away from the Timely Trips coach.

Tori peered out through the time pod's window. "The trash-bots must have turned off the magna-drag," she said.

Ana held her breath and watched as the trash-bots came out of their time coach. The one called Alpha was red with three spikes sticking up from its round head. The other was called Beta and it had a blue head shaped like a cube. They stared at the piles of scrap metal all around them.

"Error," said Alpha. "We have returned with the rubbish we dumped in first-century Rome."

"We have failed in our mission," said Beta.

"Yes, you have," came a shrill voice. Ana frowned as a golden robot in a tin-foil dress wobbled up to the trash-bots on three mechanical legs. She had orange metal hair and a fierce expression. "You tin-plated twerps! You are supposed to be getting rid of rubbish in the past – not bringing it back here."

"Sorry, Miss Stumpkin," said Alpha. "We met time travellers in Ancient Rome, just before Mount Vesuvius erupted."

"Who were they?" Miss Stumpkin demanded.

"A robot guide from Time Tours with three human children," said Beta. "They used our magna-drag to magnetise us to the trash."

"Time Tours?" Miss Stumpkin's golden face turned red. "Time Tours doesn't take tourists to visit Vesuvius in that time. That tour guide and her friends must have been snooping about! Where are they now?"

Ana gulped. She hoped the robots didn't notice the time pod among all the mangled metal wrecks.

Alpha scowled. "Their present location is unknown."

"Well, if they turn up again, they will be sorry," said Miss Stumpkin.

"Time's running out for waste disposal in this time," she went on. "Take this rubbish away to another volcano that's about to burst. If you find any more time travellers trying to interfere … deal with them."

"Affirmative," said Alpha.

"Afterwards, get back to the Timely Trips coach station and pick up the next load," Miss Stumpkin went on. "Meanwhile, I will scan for intruders in this time – just in case. Now, get going!"

Miss Stumpkin turned and wobbled away. The trash-bots stomped off, too.

Back in the time pod, Rocco wiped his brow. "Phew!" he said. "I thought they would see us hiding here for sure!"

"If only our time radio was working," said Ifan. "We could send out a call for help."

"We must travel forwards to the future," said Ana, "to your time."

"Yes, and warn the Time Police," said Tori. "They investigate problems caused by time travel."

"Let's go," said Ifan.

Tori was about to start the engines when a loud hum of power came from outside. The time pod shook and skidded into the nearest old wreck.

"The time pod is being magnetised!" Rocco shouted. "The trash-bots must have started up the magna-drag again!"

Ifan gulped. "If we stay in the time pod, we'll be dragged away like the rest of the trash here and destroyed in a volcano eruption!"

"Quickly," said Tori. "Everyone outside."

"But if we lose the time pod, we'll be stranded here!" cried Rocco.

"That's better than being sizzled up by lava," said Ana. "Tori, don't forget to switch on your anti-magnetic shield!"

Tori did so by pressing a button on her hip. Then she threw open the door. A wave of tropical heat burst in. Tori jumped out into the humid rainforest, and Rocco, Ana and Ifan scrambled after her. Above the hum of the magna-drag, the air was filled with the hoot and chirrup of unknown creatures – and then the clang and crash of heavy metal heaps colliding.

All the wrecks around them were being magnetised and dragged towards the Timely Trips coach. Trees were crushed and torn apart as old spaceships ran them down. Thorny bushes caught on rusting wings and were soon uprooted. Flying creatures squawked in fear as they took to the skies.

"Let's get out of here!" Rocco shouted, leaping over an old exhaust pipe as it slid through the grass like a metal snake.

Ana nodded. "Miss Stumpkin must have a time radio – and a time-travel machine to get out of this time. Let's try to find it."

With Tori and Ifan close behind, Rocco and Ana ran further into the thick rainforest. It was hot and humid in spite of the shade from the trees.

"Tori," said Ana, "what do you think Miss Stumpkin meant when she said, 'Time's running out for waste disposal in *this* time'?"

"She can only mean one thing," Tori said. "Sixty-six million years ago, the dinosaurs died out when a big lump of rock from outer space smashed into the world."

"A meteor," Ifan said. "I remember reading that it was nearly 15 kilometres across!"

Tori nodded. "And when it hit the Earth, the explosion threw up so much dust and dirt into the sky that it blocked out the sun for 20 years."

"A disaster that big would get rid of a whole lot of rubbish," Ana muttered.

"And here it is," said Rocco, first to reach a gap in the trees. "Look!"

Tori, Ana and Ifan crowded behind him – and all three of them gasped.

Ahead of them was a vast, deep canyon. It was jammed full of enormous, wrecked spaceships, jet planes and rocket ships, with a million other bits of junk strewn in between. This high-tech graveyard stretched on for as far as the eye could see.

Tori's satellite dish was whizzing about. "I calculate that this rubbish dump is at least 150 kilometres wide!"

"How can anyone pollute the past like this?" said Ana. "It's horrible!"

A fearsome growl sounded behind them as if in agreement. Tori and the children whirled round to find a giant, scaly monster glaring at them from the rainforest.

"D-di-dinosaur!" Ana stammered.

The dinosaur's head was the size of an armchair; its teeth were as big as bananas. Its little forearms clawed the air. It stood on tree-trunk legs, hunched over as if ready to pounce.

"Oh, dear," Tori twittered. "I regret to inform you that this is a Gorgosaurus – a meat-eating dinosaur that weighs as much as a large car!"

Rocco gulped. "In this time, dinosaurs aren't extinct," he whispered. "But I reckon we soon will be!"

For a long moment, the Gorgosaurus stared at the children and Tori, and Tori and the children stared back.

Then the Gorgosaurus opened its jaws and charged!

Ana dived between its legs and was almost whacked by its scaly tail. The dinosaur turned its head, distracted by her sudden movement. At the same time, Rocco and Ifan lifted a broken branch from the floor and waved it fiercely, trying to scare the monster away.

The Gorgosaurus bellowed its rage.

"Stay back, dinosaur!" Tori cried. "I am armed!" As she spoke, she pulled off a silver arm and stuck it between the monster's jaws! The Gorgosaurus spluttered and spat as it bit down on the metal and sparks sprayed out. It ran away into the rainforest, growling and grumbling.

"Well done, Tori," said Ana. "But now you've lost your arm."

"I can easily be repaired," said Tori. "You three cannot!"

The children gave their metal friend a grateful hug.

"What do we do now?" asked Ifan. "If Miss Stumpkin is scanning for intruders, it won't be long until she finds us!"

"And other dinosaurs might be scanning for their lunch!" added Rocco. In the distance, he could hear the sound of beasts hooting and heavy, trampling hooves. "Sounds like there's a whole herd of something heavy on the move."

"It's too risky to go looking for Miss Stumpkin's time radio right now," said Ana. "Why don't we explore that massive scrap pile? One of the old vehicles might have a time radio we can get working."

"Good idea," said Tori. "There isn't a moment to lose!"

The children and Tori started to climb down the steep slope of the canyon wall. Luckily, there was plenty of long grass and ferns to hang on to. Ana looked out across the prehistoric landscape in wonder. In the distance, she could see long-necked dinosaurs grazing on treetops and flying reptiles circling in the sky. *I can't believe I'm really seeing this!* she thought. But her eyes kept being drawn back to the ugly mountain of metal junk ahead of them. She felt so angry that anyone could want to pollute such a beautiful, unspoiled world.

Then she remembered: a meteor was coming from outer space to destroy this peace and beauty, along with three-quarters of all life on the planet. *And it will also squish us!* thought Ana with a shiver.

"Tori, how long do we have until the meteor falls?" asked Rocco.

"I don't know the exact date and time," Tori admitted. "Since Time Tours would never take tourists somewhere so dangerous, I'm not programmed with that information."

"I bet Miss Stumpkin knows!" said Ifan. "She must have a list of all the worst disasters in history ... so her trash-bots can dump junk there."

Ana nodded. "The sooner we get the Time Police here the better."

"Too right." Panting for breath, Rocco stepped on to the crumpled steel wing of a rocket. "But how will we know if any of these ships has a time radio?"

"I studied early time ships in school," said Ifan. "Their radios used special aerials shaped like lightning bolts."

"I'll keep my eyes peeled," said Ana, and Rocco gave a thumbs up.

"I will scan ahead and check the safest path through the wrecks," said Tori, her satellite dish slowly turning.

The team picked a path through the rusting landscape. Up close, they could see that the abandoned ships were heaped high with other scrap: futuristic laptops, mobiles, washing machines and other gadgets whose use Ana could only guess at.

"I wanted my world to be a cleaner place," said Ifan. "But not if it means dumping everything somewhere else!"

"Wait!" Rocco pointed through a teetering tower of broken solar panels. "That aerial there ..."

"Yes!" Tori ran forward and took a closer look. "It is attached to an old Vortex-5 time-travel machine. They came with time radios!"

Ana was about to cheer. But then an alarm went off in the distance, its long, rising note wailing a warning.

"Oh, great!" groaned Rocco. "Miss Stumpkin must know we're here in this time."

"This is very bad!" Tori twittered. "Perhaps she found my nice, shiny arm in the jaws of that Gorgosaurus!"

"We'd better check out that radio fast," said Ifan.

They ran into the old Vortex-5. The small control room was dark and rusty and falling apart. Tori tapped a big, yellow button but nothing happened.

"The batteries are flat," she said. "I shall charge them." Tori placed her remaining hand on the control panel. Everyone waited tensely. Outside, the siren went on wailing.

Finally, a silvery glow lit up the control room. "You did it!" Ana cheered.

Ifan switched on the time radio. The only sound was crackly static.

"The aerial must be broken," said Ifan, and he ducked outside to see. "Yes! Look, its audio cable has come unplugged."

"I'll climb up and plug it back in," said Rocco. "Ana, give me a leg up."

"But you'll be easy to spot up there!" Ana protested.

"I'll be as quick as I can," Rocco promised.

Ana made a cradle from her hands so her brother could push himself up. He scrambled up on to the roof of the Vortex-5 and grabbed the plastic audio cable. Rocco noticed a socket like a phone charger, blocked with dirt. "Is this where the cable goes?" he called.

"Yes!" said Ifan. "Get ready to transmit, Tori!"

Rocco brushed away the dirt and was just pushing the cable into place when a shadow fell over him.

"Look out, Rocco!" Ana yelled.

Rocco glanced up to find a giant flying creature swooping down at him. A pterosaur! Its beak was long and toothy, and its wings were like sails made of leather. With a screech, it knocked Rocco over. He almost tumbled down from the roof.

"Get away!" he shouted, kicking his legs at the pterosaur flapping above him. "Leave me alone, you overgrown turkey …"

To his surprise, the pterosaur flew away as he'd ordered, with a squawk of alarm.

Rocco beamed down at his sister. "I guess I scared it off, huh?"

Ana's eyes were full of fear as she shook her head. "It wasn't you that scared it away," she said, pointing past him across the waste tip. "Look!"

"Uh-oh," said Rocco.

Three dark discs were spinning through the air like giant frisbees, coming straight for them. As they approached, Rocco saw each frisbee had a single eye glowing white, and chunky high-tech ray-blasters on their sides.

"Robo-drones," said Ifan, clenching his teeth. "They're automatic security guards. Stumpkin must have sent them to find us."

"And they have!" said Rocco. One of the robo-drones fired its ray-blaster at the aerial – which exploded into pieces. Rocco was blown from the roof of the Vortex-5, but Ifan and Ana ran to catch him and he landed in their arms.

The three robo-drones spun more slowly as they floated down to face the children. Their ray-blasters began to glow.

Ana looked at Rocco and Ifan in horror. "They've zapped our only chance of calling for help," she said. "Now they're going to zap us!"

3 Looping the loop

Terrified, Ana closed her eyes as the three robo-drones prepared to open fire. Rocco took her hand and squeezed. "Please," said Ifan, "don't hurt us ..."

Ana heard three blasts of energy zap through the air – followed quickly by three explosions! She opened her eyes – and found the robo-drones had turned into piles of smoking metal.

"As if there wasn't enough techno-junk here already!" came a deep voice. A silver-haired man stepped out from behind the tail fin of a broken-down rocket ship.

He wore a smart white uniform with a red badge on his chest. In his hand he held a chunky ray gun. "Are you kids okay?"

"We're fine, thanks to you," said Ana. "Mr …?"

"Captain Jay Katflap," said the man.

Katflap put his ray gun in a holster at his hip. "I'm an investigator with the Time Police. Now, which one of you is Tori?"

"I AM!" Tori shot out from the Vortex-5's control room. "You heard my distress call! You came!"

Rocco grinned. "Then I *did* fix the aerial!"

"Yes, I got your signal," said Katflap. "The Time Police has been looking for you, Tori. Time Tours called us in when your time pod didn't return from Victorian London to the year 3000."

"Well, you see, we have had one or two adventures since then," Tori told him.

With Ana, Rocco and Ifan chipping in, Tori quickly explained all that they had been through.

"Very interesting," said Katflap. "We suspected that someone was transporting rubbish from the future to dump in the past. Several time ships have hit polluted patches while travelling through time – including Tori's time coach!"

"Seriously?" said Ifan.

"Time Tours mechanics reckon your coach hit a patch of old mega-oil and skidded through time," Katflap revealed. "That's what caused it to flip out of the time-flow and pick up Ana and Rocco from the 21st century."

Tori turned to Ana and Rocco and bowed. "On behalf of Time Tours, I would like to apologise once again for any inconvenience caused."

"It's Timely Trips who need to apologise," said Ana. "It's their fault, not yours."

Katflap raised an eyebrow. "You think Timely Trips are behind this rubbish-dumping plan?"

"We don't think, we *know*," said Rocco. "Those two trash-bots were riding a Timely Trips time coach."

"Yeah, Miss Stumpkin works for them," Ifan added.

"Stumpkin ... oh, yes! I've heard of her," said Katflap. "She used to be a tour guide for Timely Trips. But she kept leaving passengers behind in the past, so she was fired. Not long after that, she disappeared ... along with two Timely Trips coaches!"

"And now she's using them to dump rubbish through history," Ana said.

"So it seems," said Katflap. "I must find her base – the place from which she runs her rotten schemes. But first, I'd better call for more time officers. Come with me to my time pod, where it's safe. I landed a few hundred metres away – on a 66-million-year journey, it's hard to hit the target exactly ..."

Captain Katflap's time pod was as smart and clean as he was. Ana couldn't wait to settle down in it and feel safe again. But, as Katflap opened the door, a sinister shape came hurtling through the sky overhead.

"Look out!" Ifan shouted. "Another robo-drone!"

Katflap brought up his ray gun to knock it from the sky. But the robo-drone fired first – at Katflap's time pod! Laser beams blasted into the pod until it blew apart. The fiery explosion knocked Rocco, Ana, Tori and Ifan to the ground.

"Now we're in trouble!" said Katflap, shooting the robo-drone out of the sky. It spiralled down and crashed in the trash – but then 12 more robo-drones swooped down through the flames and smoke. "*Really* big trouble!"

"We'll never fight off all of them!" cried Rocco.

"Take cover!" yelled Ana as laser blasts started zipping all around. She and Rocco dived behind a crumpled rocket while Ifan and Tori used a sheet of metal as a shield. Katflap pulled a bronze tube from his pocket and pointed it at the robo-drones. The tube flashed with light, but the robo-drones kept coming closer ...

ZAP! Suddenly, the robo-drones seemed to jump backwards to where they were a few moments ago. Again, they advanced on Katflap and the others – and then, *ZAP!* They jumped backwards again.

Rocco stared in amazement. "It's like they're stuck on repeat."

Ifan nodded. "They're going through the same few seconds over and over."

"That's right," said Katflap. "I gave them a blast of my super-looper! Whatever it hits is trapped in a time loop – but only for a few minutes."

"But what can we do now?" said Tori. "We have no way to get more help."

"We need time to make a plan," Katflap agreed. "They know we are here. Let's hide in the rainforest."

"No way," said Rocco. "The wildlife there is hungry!"

"And I can't afford to lose another arm!" said Tori.

"We'll just have to move deeper into the dump," said Ana. "Come on!"

The children, Tori and Katflap moved quickly over the piles of scrap. They kept low so they were harder to spot. Within ten minutes, the robo-drones broke free of their time loop and came whooshing overhead, searching for intruders.

Night began to fall. A full moon rose and shone silvery light over the giant dump. The distant roars of dinosaurs and the screech of flying reptiles filled the twilight, mingling with the sinister whoosh of the robo-drones' engines as they continued their search. Then Ana noticed a strange, green glow on the jagged horizon.

"What is that?" she whispered.

"Let's find out," said Katflap. "Carefully."

The group stepped cautiously through the rusty remains of the wrecks, closing on the mysterious glow. A very large rocket ship was lying twisted and broken on its back. The glow was coming from a thick, green slime leaking through a crack in the rocket ship's side.

"Let's see what my scanner makes of it." Katflap pulled a small gadget from his belt and waved it over the dribbling split in the metal.

"Just as I feared. This is Mega-Oil 100, the dirtiest and most dangerous fuel ever invented. It's very hard to dispose of safely."

"I suppose that's why it's been dumped in the past," said Ifan. "That rocket is a Steel Enigma from the year 2900, one of the last ships to run on Mega-Oil 100."

"The fuel was banned after just 25 years," Tori explained. "Vehicles that used it went super-fast – but sometimes exploded!"

"And according to my scanner, this fuel tank is almost full," Katflap went on. "The meteor that killed the dinosaurs hit hard enough – but with so much Mega-Oil 100 lying around, the explosion will be a trillion times worse. Enough to wipe out *all* life on Earth – and split the planet in half!"

4 Prisoners!

"Let me get this straight," said Rocco. "Stumpkin and her rubbish dumping is going to destroy the Earth, 66 million years before we were even born?"

Ifan gulped. "Someone tell me he's joking."

"We Time Police investigators *never* joke!" said Katflap.

"What are we going to do?" cried Ana. "We can't let Stumpkin wreck the entire future of the planet."

Tori gave a sad shrug. "If she does, we won't know much about it. We will never have existed."

"Look out," Rocco hissed, pointing to the sky. "Robo-drones!"

Katflap bundled them into an old rocket until the spinning spy-bots had gone past.

"We must find another old wreck with a radio and call the Time Police for urgent help," said Katflap.

Ana frowned. "But those robo-drones are looking for us!"

"We'll be harder to spot if we split up," said Rocco.

"Good thinking," said Katflap. "Tori, Ifan, you explore to the north. Rocco, Ana, you go south. I'll go west by myself."

"Remember, look out for lightning-bolt aerials," said Ifan.

"And be careful!" Tori added. "We'll meet back here in an hour. The green glow of the Mega-Oil 100 will lead you back!"

Ana and Rocco picked a path through the moonlit metal landscape. They looked all around, scrambling up scrap piles and peering through the gloom, desperate to spot one of the tell-tale time radio aerials. Surely there had to be one somewhere?

"Take cover," Ana hissed suddenly. "Robo-drones!"

Rocco scrambled under the cover of a rusty rocket fin. He looked up and saw the dark, familiar shapes whizzing past the Moon, heading west.

"Katflap went that way," Rocco remembered. "I hope he hides in time …"

But the next moment, the night was lit up by blasts of bright light. The captain's cry rang out in the distance.

"Oh, no!" Ana clutched her brother's arm. "They must've got him!"

"And look," said Rocco as more flashes of light came from the north. "More of them."

"Come on!" Ana started running back towards the wreck of the Steel Enigma. "We have to help Tori and Ifan!"

But before they were even halfway there, a yell from Ifan cut through the night, quickly followed by a loud squeak from Tori.

Rocco grabbed his sister to stop her running. "Too late," he whispered.

"Miss Stumpkin wants to question the intruders," came the flat, mechanical voice of a robo-drone. "Take them to her base."

Ana and Rocco gasped to see Tori being lifted into the air by one of the rotating robo-drones. The limp bodies of Ifan and Katflap were also carried away by two more of the flying robots.

"Now there's just us," said Rocco quietly. "We can't work a time radio by ourselves, even if we find one. What are we going to do?"

"Keep watching," said Ana, trying to keep their friends' faint figures in sight. "See where they're being taken ..."

The drones dropped down out of sight on the other side of the rainforest.

"Great," said Rocco in frustration. "Now we just have to think of a way to save Katflap, Tori and Ifan from a load of flying robots and their grumpy boss."

"Let's think while we move," said Ana. "Come on!"

* * *

On the edge of the rainforest, Ifan woke up and found he could not move. The warmth of the tropical night had been replaced with freezing cold air-con.

He was tied up on a seat on board a dusty, old coach.

A Timely Trips coach, thought Ifan.

Tori was strapped down in the seat beside him. Captain Katflap was a prisoner in the seat in front, still asleep.

"Are you all right, Ifan?" Tori asked quietly. "On behalf of Time Tours, I would like to apologise for this unexpected visit to a rival tour operator's coach."

"It's not your fault," said Ifan. "Where and when are we?"

Tori's satellite dish spun slowly about. "It is still 66 million years ago," she said. "We have been taken to the other side of Miss Stumpkin's illegal waste tip."

"And it will be a one-way journey!" came a harsh, electronic voice as Miss Stumpkin wobbled into the coach on her three legs. "You were fools to come snooping round here."

"The past belongs to everyone," said Tori. "That is the first law of time travel. Every tour guide knows that." She narrowed her robotic eyes. "But you're not a tour guide any more, are you? Now you take trash for trips instead of passengers."

"I'm simply using the past to make things cleaner in our own time," said Miss Stumpkin. "Plus, the rubbish companies pay me loads more than Timely Trips ever did."

"And in return you get rid of the worst of their junk," said Ifan. "By dumping it in the past!"

"We know you're planning to use the meteor that wiped out the dinosaurs to pulverise all that junk out there," said Tori. "But one of those wrecks has a full tank of Mega-Oil 100!"

"Does it?" Miss Stumpkin shrugged. "So what?"

"So, that stuff is super-explosive!" said Ifan. "It could split the Earth apart."

"Stop trying to trick me," Miss Stumpkin said.

"It's true! And the Time Police know it, too." Tori nodded to Captain Katflap, who was still out cold. "And if the world *isn't* blown up, you'll be caught and sent to prison for polluting the past!"

Miss Stumpkin glared at Tori. "If the Time Police know, why haven't they come here to catch me? How come this snoozing specimen is the only officer here?"

Ifan gulped. "Er, they're giving you a chance to surrender," he fibbed quickly. "Give yourself up and let us go – then we can all work together to clean up this mess before the meteor hits!"

"No way," Miss Stumpkin said. "I don't think this investigator had time to tell the Time Police anything. Otherwise, they'd be all over the place. And that is bad news for you – because the meteor is going to crash into the Earth in just four hours!"

5 Unexpected callers

Meanwhile, Rocco and Ana were moving through the rainforest beside the waste dump, making their way to Miss Stumpkin's base. Dawn was breaking. They had no idea that the massive meteor would hit in just four hours' time!

"How are we going to rescue Tori, Ifan and Katflap from Miss Stumpkin?" Rocco asked, still trying to think of ideas.

"We need a distraction," said Ana, jumping over a stream. "If we can find a way to keep Miss Stumpkin busy, we can sneak into her base and save the others."

"Yeah! And use her time radio to call the Time Police!" said Rocco. "They can come and take away the Mega-Oil 100 before anything bad happens ..."

Suddenly, a huge, scaly face as big as a boulder appeared from behind some nearby bushes.

Two horns curved out from its head like swords, and a third, stumpy horn sat on its nose. Rocco yelled in surprise. "Look out!" he shouted, heading for a tree. "It's a triceratops or something! It'll eat us!"

"Triceratops was a plant eater," said Ana, backing away slowly. "I'm more worried that it'll trample us into mush!"

"Quick, climb a tree!" Rocco said, shinning up the nearest trunk. Ana quickly followed him.

The triceratops turned its head and hooted. Many calls came back in answer.

"Oh, wow, there are loads of them!" said Rocco, staring out at the huge beasts from his spot in the branches of the tree. "Look out, Ana!"

Ana clung to a tree branch as more three-horned monsters stomped from the bushes. Each was as big as a monster truck! "I'm staying here till the herd goes past," she said.

"Too right," said Rocco. But then he saw a dark shape spinning through the sky. "Uh-oh. Robo-drone!" Quickly, he retreated down the tree and called to Ana. "Don't worry, I don't think it saw me."

A blast of light sizzled through the leaves beside them and the children cried out as they fell to the ground.

Ana groaned. "The drone *totally* saw you!"

Another energy beam shot past and struck a tree.

The triceratops hooted with alarm. More of the giant animals burst from the bushes.

"Run!" Ana yelled, *eyes wide with panic*.

Rocco was already charging away through the bushes, terrified of being squashed flat. "You know where they're pushing us, don't you!" he panted. "Towards Stumpkin's base!"

"You're right," said Ana, running faster to keep up with her brother. "I said we needed a distraction – and I reckon we might just have found it!"

* * *

Back in Miss Stumpkin's coach, Ifan felt numb with horror. "Four hours until the meteor hits?" he cried. "We've got to get rid of that Mega-Oil 100 before then!"

"Yes, we must," said Tori. "This is an emergency, Miss Stumpkin!"

"I'm not falling for your pathetic trick," said Miss Stumpkin. "Now I know you're no danger to me, I can dump you outside with the rest of the rubbish and let the meteor take care of you."

Ifan stared at her. "That's murder!"

"I prefer to think of it as waste disposal." With an electronic giggle, she lifted the tied-up Ifan from his seat and dragged him along the coach gangway to the doors. "I can't hang around in any case," Miss Stumpkin went on. "I've got more rubbish from the future to take care of."

Ifan gasped as Miss Stumpkin threw him outside into the hot, wet morning. A minute later, both Tori and Captain Katflap lay beside him in the dirty, dusty earth.

"Ugh," groaned Katflap, stirring beside Tori. "What happened?"

"You lost, police officer!" said Miss Stumpkin. She looked up and saw a robo-drone flying towards them above the nearby rainforest. "Aha! It seems my robot servants have found your two little friends! Just in time for you to say goodbye …"

"Wait," Ifan whispered. "The ground is trembling."

"That pounding sound," said Katflap. "I thought it was in my head, but it's real …"

Suddenly, Ana and Rocco emerged from the rainforest, dirty and sweaty and panting for breath.

Miss Stumpkin scowled at them. "Don't move!" she shouted.

"Wrong!" said Rocco as the pounding sound grew louder. "*Do* move! Right now!"

"You've got company coming!" Ana panted. Then she and Rocco ran aside as the saplings at the edge of the rainforest were flattened by 20 charging triceratops! The dinosaurs ran on in blind panic, scared by the stinging blasts from the robo-drone firing its way through the trees. Miss Stumpkin and her coach were directly in their path!

"Eek!" Miss Stumpkin ran for the coach at a wonky gallop. "Robo-drones," she cried. "Stop those dinosaurs!"

More mechanical monsters swooped down from the skies, firing at the dinosaurs. But the animals were protected by their tough, scaly hides – and the zaps just made them angrier.

Panic-stricken, Miss Stumpkin jumped into the driver's seat of her coach. But before she could take off, the front row of dinosaurs lowered their huge, horned heads and butted into the vehicle's side!

There was a boom like thunder as the coach was thrown over and landed on its back. More charging dinosaurs either ran into it or climbed over it, leaving dents and cracked windows where they passed.

Some smashed into the underside of the coach, sending sparks flying from the time engines as they tried to force the vehicle out of their path. The robo-drones went on firing, but they were zapping the coach by accident as they tried to hit the dinosaurs.

"Stop, drones!" Stumpkin yelled. "Deactivate!"

The robo-drones switched off and dropped from the sky, bouncing off the vehicle's battered bodywork. Finally, as the last beast charged past, it seemed Miss Stumpkin's coach could take no more. Flames burst out from its base, and its door was blown off its hinges by a fiery explosion.

Miss Stumpkin was thrown from the coach and landed face-down in the mud, sparking and smoking. "Noooooo," she wailed, her voice growing lower as her power ran down. "This ... is ... *rubbish* ..."

She fell quiet.

"Wow," said Ana, staring at the overturned coach and the smouldering Miss Stumpkin. "Those triceratops almost did that to *us*."

"Actually, triceratops didn't live in Mexico," said Tori. "Those animals were a similar breed called *ko-a-WEY-la-SEH-ra-tops*—"

"Who cares what they were called!" groaned Ifan. "Miss Stumpkin said the meteor will strike the Earth in less than four hours."

"*What?*" cried Rocco, Ana and Katflap together.

"We must do something," said Katflap. "Ana, quickly – there's a heat saw in my belt. It will cut through these plastic ropes."

Ana pulled the tool from his belt. She pressed a button and a blade of light slid out. Straight away, she started sawing at Tori's bonds. "Maybe Stumpkin's time radio is still working," said Ana. "We can call for help."

Flexing her metal muscles, Tori broke through the melting straps. "I shall find out," she said and ran into the smoky coach to see.

Ana quickly cut through Katflap's straps, then moved on to Ifan. The captain got to his feet as Tori came back out.

"Well?" he asked.

"I regret to report that the controls have all burned out," said Tori. "We can't get help, and we're stranded here – on a doomed planet!"

6 Doomsday

"All Timely Trips technology is the same," Tori groaned, nudging Miss Stumpkin with her foot. "Like her – it's cheap and easily broken!"

"But technology can be fixed," said Katflap. "I'll make sure Miss Stumpkin is repaired later, so she can pay for her crimes. But, Tori, we *must* get that time radio working again. Now!"

"It's completely wrecked," Tori told him. "But there's a chance we can get the coach engines going again. By using circuits from me and Miss Stumpkin, I can get some of the systems back online."

"Fix that wreck?" Rocco didn't look convinced. "With only one arm?"

"She must," said Katflap. "It's our last and only hope of saving the planet ... and ourselves."

"I'll help you, Tori," said Ifan.

"Thank you," said Tori. Together, they carried Miss Stumpkin back on board the battered coach.

"Rocco, let's go with Captain Katflap to collect the Mega-Oil 100," said Ana. "If Tori and Ifan *can* get the coach working, we can load it on board and get out of here before the meteor hits."

"That's a big 'if'," said Rocco. "But, sure. Let's go."

He followed Ana and Katflap as they ran back into the rainforest. Time was running out and his stomach was churning. *Three kids, a time cop and a one-armed robot*, he thought. *And we're Earth's only hope!*

Rocco, Ana and Katflap ran to the Steel Enigma and stared at the Mega-Oil 100 glowing inside the rocket's fuel tanks. "How do we deal with it?" Rocco asked.

"It's too dangerous to touch the oil itself," said Katflap.

"What about your heat saw?" said Ana. "Maybe we can cut out the fuel tank."

"And then load the tank full of Mega-Oil 100 into the coach!" Katflap smiled. "That is a good idea."

Rocco nodded. "But is your little flame thing going to be strong enough?"

"Not on its own," said Katflap. "See if you can find some other tools. We need to slice through a lot of metal. We'll have to work like we've never worked before."

"I just hope Tori and Ifan can get Stumpkin's coach going," said Rocco.

Ana found an old toolbox strapped inside a crashed aircraft.

She didn't recognise any of the tools, but Katflap pulled out a large laser burner. It shone a beam of light that could cut through metal; the battery was almost flat, but it was better than nothing. Rocco found a piece of flat metal with a jagged edge. Katflap gave Rocco the heat saw and used the scrap of metal himself.

The three of them got busy trying to cut through the fuel tanks. Sweat was pouring down Ana's back, and it wasn't just down to working in the heat. She knew that, right now, a giant rock was hurtling towards the Earth.

History showed that it had struck the very spot they stood on, 66 million years before she'd been born.

Sixty-six million years ago, she thought, *but also, any minute now!* Time travel was crazy. And also terrifying.

Ana tried to stay calm and work as quickly as she could. But as the hours passed, fear gripped her harder and tighter. There was still a lot of the rocket's side left to cut through! And no sign of Tori and Ifan.

She saw Rocco wiping his eyes. "Just sweat," he said quickly. "I'm not crying."

"Course not," said Ana. "Why don't you try to find another tool? My laser burner's battery is so low it could hardly burn toast!"

Rocco nodded and scrambled over a slope of rubbish, just out of sight.

Ana looked at Katflap. "How long do we have left?"

He looked at her and sighed. "If Stumpkin was right about the time, we have around ten minutes before the meteor hits."

Ana swallowed hard. She wanted to cry. Had all their efforts been for nothing?

"Hey!" Rocco shouted from behind the slope. "I see the coach! It's coming. *It's coming!*"

Ana and Katflap grinned wildly at each other. Then Ana dashed off up the rubbish slope to see for herself. Sure enough, the battered coach was rumbling over the uneven ground towards them.

"You got the coach moving!" cheered Rocco as the coach pulled up. "Great work, guys!"

But Ifan didn't look happy as he climbed out to join them. Tori followed him. There were holes in her side and in her right leg where she'd taken parts from herself to help with the repairs.

"There's a slight problem," Tori squeaked. "The time engines should work, just about – but they will take at least another 15 minutes to warm up."

Ana felt her heart sink into her shoes. "But ... there's less than ten minutes until the meteor hits!"

Rocco clutched his stomach. "And we haven't cut out the rocket's fuel tank yet."

"What are we going to do?" cried Ifan.

No one spoke. Then Tori trilled in horror, "Look! Up in the sky!"

A point of burning light had appeared in the cloudless blue.

"It's the meteor!" Rocco screamed. "We're too late!"

7 A stitch in time

Ana stared up in horror as, with horrible speed, the meteor grew bigger and brighter. A shadow started to spread over the land.

"The super-looper!" Ana shouted suddenly. "Katflap, you used it to trap those robo-drones in a time loop yesterday. You can use it now to stop the meteor landing!"

"Put a whole meteor in a time loop?" Katflap frowned. "It's too big a rock to hold for long, especially travelling at that speed."

"At least give it a go!" Rocco urged him. "There's nothing else we can do."

Katflap pulled the tube from his belt and held it to the sky. The meteor was still hurtling towards them, impossible to miss. The sky began to fill with its burning bulk until it blotted out everything. The air sizzled with fierce heat.

Ana held her breath, too frightened even to think. The giant rock would land any second, it already seemed close enough to touch …

Then, suddenly, the meteor seemed to jump backwards and became a burning point of light again. It screeched closer, its fiery shadow spreading across the sky … then, again, it disappeared and retreated to the high heavens before starting to fall once more.

"It worked!" Rocco cheered. "Fantastic!"

"It won't work for long," Katflap warned them. "This super-looper is running low on power. I can only stop the meteor for another few minutes at most."

"Tori, you're strong," said Ana. "Can you help us take out the rocket's fuel tank? Then we can carry it aboard the coach and take the Mega-Oil 100 away with us."

"I can try," said Tori. "But the engines won't warm up before we run out of time."

"What if you use some of the Mega-Oil 100?" said Rocco. "That stuff's the strongest fuel ever made, isn't it? Maybe the engines won't need to warm up so much."

"Brilliant, Rocco!" Katflap grinned. "It's risky ... but at least there's a chance!"

The meteor was moving a fraction closer every time it fell, like a dog straining to bite a postman. Katflap fired the super-looper again, and the meteor fell back a little way – but not as far as before.

"We'd better get to work!" said Ifan.

The shadow of the meteor loomed ever larger over them all. The heat in the air was incredible. Ana thought she might melt! She and Rocco used their weakening tools to cut upwards from the base of the rusting rocket, while Tori used her single arm to karate chop her way downwards.

"Keep going," Tori encouraged them. "When we meet in the middle, the fuel tank should be free and we can pull it away!"

Meanwhile, Katflap had carefully scooped up some
Mega-Oil 100 with a long piece of metal. Ifan helped
him add it to the engines.

"Only a tiny drop at a time," Katflap whispered.
"Otherwise we might blow up the whole coach."

"That might happen anyway," said Ifan quietly.

Katflap nodded. "We have to take the chance."

The meteor was still falling over and over, faster
and faster. It was now so close to the ground that
its shadow covered everything. Ana felt she could
almost reach up on tiptoes and touch it.

"Fuel is loaded!" called Katflap.

"I'm going to test the engines again!" said Ifan, climbing aboard. "Just like you showed me, Tori."

Finally, with a squeal and the grinding of tearing metal, the fuel tank started to come away from the rocket.

"Catch it, Tori!" Ana shouted.

"I only have one arm!" wailed Tori. Ana and Rocco helped her support it, and Katflap raced over to lend his strength. The meteor hung over them, hardly slipping back in time at all. Any moment now it would hit!

"The engines!" yelled Ifan as a sudden hum of power rattled the coach. "I think they're taking the new fuel! The power is increasing."

"We must get this fuel tank aboard!" squealed Tori. "Ifan, open up the luggage compartment!"

"And blast that meteor with the super-looper again!" said Ana.

Ifan scrambled out of the coach and grabbed the super-looper from Katflap's belt. He fired it once more at the meteor, which hardly flickered.

"Out of juice," Ifan groaned, and prised open the storage panels on the battered coach. Then he helped Ana, Rocco, Tori and Katflap slide the fuel tank inside.

"Done it!" Rocco shouted, slamming the cover shut.

"Now, everyone into the coach!" yelled Katflap.

The coach was shaking with power as Ana led the scramble to get on board. Tori slid into the driver's seat beside Miss Stumpkin's dented body. "Here goes," she called. "Activating time jump ... now!"

Rocco held his breath. Through the cracked windows, he could see every detail of the giant, burning rock above them that was set to obliterate everything for hundreds of kilometres around. The hum of power inside the coach rose in pitch, then dipped and wobbled.

"Come on!" Katflap shouted.

"I can't push the engines too hard," Tori shouted back. "They might explode!"

Rocco looked at his sister. Ana smiled bravely back at him. Quietly, without anything being said, they held hands.

Finally, the hum of power grew stronger, louder. The coach shook and lifted into the air. The world outside began to grow hazy.

"It's working!" cried Rocco. "We're taking off!"

"Next stop, the year 3000!" said Ana, and everyone cheered.

Finally, the meteor struck. The impact was strong enough to make the whole world ripple and shake. Rock was turned to liquid. Billions of tons of dirt and dust were thrown up into the sky. Heat scorched all life in that part of Mexico into shadows.

But no human eyes or robot vision saw it happen. The time coach, and the deadly fuel it carried, were already millions of years away …

8 Home time

It caused quite a stir when the battered Timely Trips coach appeared in Time Tours' clean and tidy garage. Cleaning robots and security drones rushed to the scene to investigate.

"It's all right," said Captain Katflap, staggering outside. "This coach is here on official Time Police business – and it's carrying true heroes!"

For Ana and Rocco, the next day passed in a daze. Katflap made sure they were treated like VIPs in the year 3000. He had them whisked away to a special hotel where robot servants brought them drinks and food in amazing flavours they had never tasted before! They looked out at the future world through large windows but couldn't see much for the thick, black smog blowing past like clouds.

"There is so much pollution here," said Ana sadly.

"Maybe," said Rocco. "But I still can't wait to explore the year 3000!"

"Sorry. That's not going to happen," Katflap told him. "It's one thing to travel back in time. But no one should know the future."

"Oh!" said Ana. "But why can't we?"

"You could learn things you were never meant to know," Katflap told her. "Things that might change how you live in your own time."

"When are we going back?" asked Rocco.

"Later today," said Katflap.

"Thank you," said Ana. "I'm really starting to miss our friends and family."

"Can we see Tori and Ifan again – to say goodbye?" asked Rocco.

Katflap smiled. "Of course."

Tori was the first to visit them in the hotel. She was already fully repaired with a brand-new arm, and her silver skin shone with polish.

"Greetings!" she squeaked. "On behalf of Time Tours, I hope you are enjoying your stay—"

"Oh, Tori!" Rocco broke in. "On behalf of me and Ana, shut up and have a hug!"

Ana put her arms around Tori. "We'll miss you," she said. "You're the best tour guide ever. Past, present or future!"

"I agree," said Ifan, stepping into the room behind her. He was wearing a smart blue jumpsuit, and looking neater than Rocco and Ana had ever seen him. "And this is the best *day* ever, too! Once Miss Stumpkin was repaired, she confessed everything she did to the Time Police. They are travelling back through time to arrest her trash-bots and clean up the messes they've helped her make through history."

"The Mega-Oil 100 has also been properly disposed of," said Tori. "It won't pose a danger to anyone, ever again."

"That's great news," said Rocco. "I hope they'll lock up the people who paid Stumpkin to dump their rubbish."

"They're already under arrest!" Ifan revealed. "Best of all, Katflap says that, because of the part I played in saving the world, me and my family will be moved to a bigger and better apartment. It's a dream come true – I'll have more space at last!"

"Brilliant," said Ana. "You definitely deserve it."

"And this whole experience has made me see that the Earth deserves a lot more care," Ifan went on. "I'm going to learn all I can about how to make our planet a greener, cleaner place."

"We'll be doing our bit, too, when we get back home," said Rocco. "Reusing things. Recycling. Choosing technology that doesn't cause waste."

"Because otherwise, the Earth might not even *reach* the year 3000!" Ana said.

"Teamwork is what it takes," said Rocco with a grin. "And we're a pretty amazing team."

"Now it is time to say goodbye," said Tori sadly, as a time pod appeared in the middle of the hotel room. "Next stop, the 21st century! I will drop you off just a few moments after you were scooped up by my time coach."

"We won't forget you, will we?" asked Ana. "I don't want to forget any of our adventures."

"You won't," said Tori. "But ... keep what happened to yourselves."

Ifan laughed. "I don't think anyone would believe you anyway!"

Rocco and Ana waved goodbye to Ifan, then got inside the time pod. Tori worked the controls with a smile. "Let's hope it's a smoother journey this time."

Soon, just as Tori had said, the time pod appeared on the same stretch of pavement that Ana and Rocco had vanished from over a week ago.

"Goodbye ... my friends," said Tori.

Ana turned to wave one last time. But the time pod had already gone.

Together they finished the walk back home. They couldn't stop smiling as they opened their familiar front door and saw their mum in the kitchen.

"Look at the state of you both!" cried Mum, looking at their dirty school uniforms. "How did you get so grubby at school ...?"

Rocco swapped a secret smile with his sister. "I wish I had *time* to tell you, Mum!"

"But the truth is, it's ancient history," Ana added. "Is dinner ready? We're starving!"

Chat about the book

1 Read page 27. What caused the Time Tours coach to end up in the 21st century?

2 The author called Chapter 1, 'Prehistoric Peril'. What other word could have been used that is similar to 'peril'?

3 Go to page 15. Why did Rocco suggest they were soon going to be extinct?

4 What do we learn about the character Captain Katflap in Chapter 3?

5 Why is 'Doomsday' a good name for Chapter 6?

6 Look at page 18. Why are the words, 'I can't believe I'm really seeing this!' in italics?

7 What do you think the author wanted Rocco, Ana and Ifan to learn from their trip back in time?

8 Why do you think the author chose the names, 'Captain Katflap' and 'Miss Stumpkin'? Do you know any other stories that have interesting character names?